About the Author

Alison Huckvale is an avid Leicester City and Tottenham Hotspur football supporter, depending on which team is doing well! She has recently hung up her own football boots after many years of coaching and managing football at grassroots. This is Alison's second publication, her first being *The Tortoise of Hope*. She is thirty years happily married to David with two independent daughters, Olivia and Holly-Mae. To complete the family are Bella and Koko—two adorable Schnoodles.

Alison enjoys art, painting and exploring different mediums, along with her more recent hobbies—crocheting and playing the ukulele—but not at the same time! She is the proud owner of 28 implants, having braved the option to fill her mouth with healthier teeth, but more importantly, to allow her to smile for the first time in fifty years.

Dedication

To my daughters Olivia and Holly-Mae, who gave me the inspiration to keep on writing even during times when resilience was more important.

Alison Huckvale

THE CHAMELEON OF CHOICE

AUSTIN MACAULEY PUBLISHERS®
LONDON * CAMBRIDGE * NEW YORK * SHARJAH

Copyright © Alison Huckvale 2025

The right of Alison Huckvale to be identified as author of this work has been asserted by the author in accordance with sections 77 and 78 of the Copyright, Designs and Patents Act 1988.

All rights reserved. No part of this publication may be reproduced, stored in a retrieval system, or transmitted in any form or by any means, electronic, mechanical, photocopying, recording, or otherwise, without the prior permission of the publishers.

Any person who commits any unauthorised act in relation to this publication may be liable to criminal prosecution and civil claims for damages.

A CIP catalogue record for this title is available from the British Library.

ISBN 9781035877935 (Paperback)
ISBN 9781035877942 (ePub e-book)

www.austinmacauley.com

First Published 2025
Austin Macauley Publishers Ltd®
1 Canada Square
Canary Wharf
London
E14 5AA

Acknowledgements

First of all, I would like to thank my family and friends who have continued to share and support life's journey—especially during times of poor physical and mental health, when I've had to dig deep for positivity. Collectively, you have all given me the strength to complete my second book of poems and the confidence to share my artwork too.

I would like to thank my friends Jackie Wilkinson and Elaine Kirt, who have spent hours reading and editing my poems and talking about their deeper meaning and the audience my book aims to support. You have both understood how 'words' written have captured memories from much younger years.

I am thankful to my friend Lydia Boardman, who kindly turned my drawings and paintings into an electronic form. The vast majority of the pieces of art that accompany the poems were completed by myself.

I am grateful to my friend and artist Deb Birks for her acrylic painting that accompanies my poem entitled What is Gender?

I am also grateful to Rose Allinson—Proprietor/Artist—The Art Studio and Ten2 Gallery in Hinckley, Leicestershire, for illustrating and painting the chameleon that adorns the front cover of my book.

I would also like to thank Kirsty Whitlow for introducing and allowing me to be artistic with and without a paintbrush; using both watercolours and acrylics alongside pastels, chalks and inks. Having spent the last three years attending classes taught by Kirsty, I now have the confidence to share my final images, which I have used to illustrate poems in this book.

Likewise, I'd like to thank my friends at Cosby Crafters, who has not only shown me how to crochet but also the benefits of crocheting to calm the mind. Participating in Cosby Yarn Bomb gave me a sense of purpose and belonging.

Attending both the art classes and crocheting sessions have been pivotal and hugely beneficial in promoting and maintaining positive mental health, but most of all, classes are a place to chat, laugh and encourage each other.

Finally, I would like to thank the NHS for keeping me well and giving me the confidence to take each day as it comes.

Table of Contents

Background Information	13
Preface	14
Sick	15
Chameleon Behaviour—Out in the Open	17
My Motivator	19
Alive or Exist?	20
Pain Registers	21
My Wheelchair and I	22
Who Do I Wake Up As?	24
The Chameleon Salute	25
Back and Forth	27
What My Body Needs Most	28
My Autumn Dungarees	30
Biscuit Tin	31
Feeling the Frost	32
Simply 'Because'	33
Leaving by the Back Door	34
Hairdryer in the City	36
Transition	37
Toxicity	38
My Brain is a Compass	39
Compensatory Bandages	40
A Little Bit of Me…	42
Advice from a Pencil on How to Diet	43
Still—Who? What? Where? Why? When? The Teacher Asked.	44
Life is a Tapestry	45
Scared	47
Poetic Emancipation	49
ALONE	50
Darkened Space	51

Medium-sized	53
The Indigo Starseed	54
My Social Chameleon	55
It Smelt of Love	56
Colours—Which One Am I Today?	57
What Can 'Red' Do?	58
One Hundred Years Ago…	59
For Which Environment?	60
My Awkward Aura	61
Old Oak Tree	62
Can You Erase the Future?	63
The Difference Amongst Moons	64
Changing Places	65
Alien Brand	66
Pretending	67
Cargo	68
The Raceless Race	69
Empty Echoes	70
Born into a New Form	71
The Sum of Me!	72
Simply Anything	74
Canary Girls	75
My History…	77
What is Gender?	78
Trials and Tribulations That a New Year Brings	79
To Do One's Best	80
Contented	**81**
Aesthetic Taste Buds	83
What is ART?	84
How to Paint a Picture Postcard of Paradise	85
Colours I Believe In	86
My Purple Dm's	87
You'll never believe what I can see	89

Mellow Yellow	90
My Name is Colin, the Chameleon	91
Factory Made	92
Springtime	93
I Saw The Lambs…After a poem by Thomas Hardy: I Watched a Blackbird	94
Lambing	95
'Skeggy' Memories	96
Richmond Caravan Park, Skegness	97
Bantering Bees	98
My Maldive Man	99
Heaven's Reflection	100
My Interpretation – What is 'belief'?	101
Random Mat	102
Down the Rabbit Hole	103
Blackbird	105
Freedom	106
The 'Box'	107
Quaker Haikus	108
Gardencraft	109
My Summary of Jamaica	110
Inspired By My Own Recovery	111
Gender Fluid	112
If I Had Any Superpower, I Would Want the Power to Control Smiling	113
Blackberry Picking	114
Nova, Nova – Supernova	115
A Debut Selection of Poems by Poppy	**117**
Fears	118
The Rain	119
The Reason	120
Things Only I Will Ever Know	121
Trauma Is My Devil	122
Your Eyes	123

Background Information

Cauda Equina Syndrome (CES) occurs when there is dysfunction of multiple lumbar and sacral nerve roots of the cauda equina (the tail end of the spinal cord). It is a surgical emergency, but if not diagnosed or treated in time, it cuts off both motor and sensory functions in the legs, including damaged bladder/bowel control.

Post-traumatic stress disorder (PTSD) is a psychiatric disorder that occurs when people experience or witness a traumatic event, series of events or set of circumstances. People with PTSD have intense, disturbing thoughts and feelings related to their experience that last long after the traumatic event has ended. They may relive the event through flashbacks or nightmares; they may feel sadness, fear or anger; and they may feel detached or estranged from other people. People with PTSD may avoid situations or people that remind them of the traumatic event, and they may have strong negative reactions to something as ordinary as a loud noise or an accidental touch.

Complex post-traumatic stress disorder (complex PTSD or C-PTSD) is a condition where you experience some symptoms of PTSD along with some additional symptoms, such as: difficulty controlling your emotions and feeling very angry or distrustful towards the world.

Emotionally unstable personality disorder (EUPD) is the rapid and extreme changes in mood, as well as the negative feelings it creates in yourself and towards others. It is the pervasive instability of interpersonal relationships, self-image, mood and impulsive behaviour.

High-functioning ADHD is when you experience severe symptoms but have developed 'workarounds' to carry on with daily tasks and responsibilities; your symptoms are mild and you're able to function with minimal impairment or symptoms are greatly impairing in some areas but you're highly functional in others.

I have all of these conditions, but rather than address any blame to them, I simply say I'm having an 'Alison' moment!

Preface

The connection between creativity and mental illness has been widely debated. Drawing, painting or writing are among several 'arts' in the form of therapy that allow someone to disconnect mentally and enjoy colour. Just as a chameleon chooses its colours, they change in response to their feelings, so this analogy with a human is quite striking.

The phrase 'Wearing your true colours' means what lies underneath our skin transforms who we are and is impossible to paint over. Fascinated with the correlation between colour and emotions, Alison explores art as the creation of something bigger; that something that affects who we are and the way we choose to live.

The creative process helps people resolve conflicts and problems, develop interpersonal skills, manage behaviour, reduce stress, increase self-esteem and self-awareness, and achieve insight. Much of the background reading and research Alison read connecting creativity and mental illness came from the publication edited by James C. Kaufman (2014) *Creativity and Mental Illness,* Cambridge University Press, Cambridge, England.

The underlying phenomena of creativity and mental illness are multifaceted and interwoven. Most recent studies have led to something resembling a consensus that links creativity and mental illness as a genuine, pervasive and timeless phenomenon with decided roots that most often take the form of manic-depressive illness or related types of mood disorders[1].

Aristotle wrote that all of the creative geniuses of time were 'inclined toward insanity'—the notion that creative genius and 'madness'; are linked; famous examples being Vincent Van Gogh and John Nash (Nobel prize-winning mathematician).

Only through research did Alison establish why chameleons are not suitable as pets; further reading will explain why. The biggest decision she faced when putting together her collection of poems was how to link them to one of the three phases we see in a chameleon; that of being sick, scared or contented. It was also important Alison captured the choices humans make depending upon the environment surrounding them.

At the end of the book, Alison introduces Poppy aged twelve, who listens to how poetry has and continues to help Alison, to then begin to use poetry as a way to express herself when talking didn't seem an option.

---

[1] Becker, G. (2001) 'The association of creativity and psychopathology; its cultural-historical origins,' *Creativity Research Journal,* **13**, 45-53.

Sick

Chameleon Behaviour — Out in the Open

I'm misunderstood
I'm emotionally unstable (EU)
I have a personality disorder (PD)
I have abandonment issues
I do not feel worthy
All labels rather than actions.

Frame me as a chameleon.
I'm predictable
living within my own skin.
Relationships may be sporadic,
mood changes galore,
naked pornographic,
revealing more truth to explore.

It's important I learn routines.
I necessitate passion.
I have to grasp displacement
to find safety when faced with trauma.
Loving myself is mandatory whilst
realistic boundaries murmur.

As a chameleon, I have three life phases –
the sick, the scared, and the contented.
Each phase dovetailing,
so it's important I learn to relax.
I must take hold of branches with measured control
ensure the area surrounding me is parallax.

Fronting the **sick chameleon**
I try and hide my sickness.
The most obvious sign of trouble and
I'll close up my eyes, sink them into my face
and show you darker colours in my skin.
You may even notice my nose pointing up in the air.

Fronting the **scared chameleon**
I take a firm grip with my coiled tail,
and show you the brightest of colours.
I puff out my chest to impose authority,
I show off my gaping jaws;
I'll raise my front leg into a protective position
all because I feel threatened

Fronting the **contented chameleon**
I'm relaxed, but alert!
I have a powerful grip on the branches I perch on.
If disturbed I will quickly slink away into foliage.
I will continue to scan the area—eyes wide open,
balancing with my coiled tail under me; and
you will get used to my resting colours.

I was born to feel the pain of generations past as
I attempt to heal those long-felt wounds.
I need to accept I am powerful and made of greatness—
a mantra I need to regularly rehearse.
I ruminate with the intimacy of my sporadic emotions.
I know my triggers and am self-aware,
recognising there will always be ups and downs.
I need firm foundations and solid support,
to keep a positive outlook on life;
I'm not that different to a chameleon you see,
the only difference is they live in a tree.

My Motivator

Disability is my motivator
to achieve the impossible.
I ask people not to pity me
but champion me instead.
Difficulties I encounter may frustrate me
so a changed perception is necessary.
Determination is a must,
patience a virtue.

Alive or Exist?

I am alive but don't recognise myself.
In my conscience, I merely exist,
I question my being.
To what extent can I see happiness?
Do I feel happy?
I may appear content with my own surroundings,
so my family say I am well and truly alive
but being alive is so much more than breathing.
I exist amongst my surroundings,
but being alive requires emotions;
those that I do not have!

Pain Registers

This poem was written at a time when my husband was getting life-changing surgery and I was left at home with my mental health; self-harm was my mechanism to cope.

His pain would register nine out of ten,
whilst my pain didn't register.
Simply wouldn't register!
Pain can be visible in a bandaged limb;
medication taken to reduce the spoken din,
whilst my pain didn't register.
Simply wouldn't register!

His pain has a name;
something tangible to blame,
whilst my pain had risen its ugly head again.
A pain without a name—just shame.
He's now able to control the pain,
whilst my pain didn't register.
Simply wouldn't register!

Intervention should also improve his pain.
As I looked on—waiting, waiting again.
Waiting for the call I had been waiting for,
regardless of the fact that I had hit the floor.
My mental pain takes me to unwelcomed places,
amongst crowds of less familiar faces.
My pain still failing to register.
Simply wouldn't register!

By the time they have addressed his pain,
I had lost all my faculties again.
At what point, should I have said 'No'?
'No' to the illness's addiction, so
the trigger fired and I'm left to bleed
this desire and need in the life I lead.
Still, my pain didn't register!
Simply wouldn't register!
That need to feel pain
pain, pain, enough? Again.

My Wheelchair and I

Dialogue between myself and the local theatre company—debating what is politically correct.

My wheelchair cannot speak!
So why do people talk to it?
It is me who makes the choices.
My wheelchair cannot walk,
yet it owns my legs—
stability and comfort so important.
My wheelchair is my legs!

Today I took a phone call from the local theatre asking if my wheelchair wanted a seat or a space.

"My wheelchair is a chair, so it doesn't need a seat," I curtly replied *"Okay, so we will take out two seats."*
When I ask why?
I'm told *"because it can be a bit of a nuisance if the chair is too big"*.
So not a case of the space being too small, it's if it fits in!
Now my wheelchair is a nuisance.
"You will need to ask someone if you need the disabled toilet!"
When I ask "Why?" as I have my own radar key to open it.
They respond—*"We've had to put another lock on it because we've had a bit of trouble with visitors misusing it!"*
So basically, I need to ask someone to use a toilet where I could potentially be locked in!
How many other visitors will be asking to use the toilet before they go?
And what's all this misuse about?
I'd like to see or hear more about it.
Next, they will be putting CCTV in there or providing a chaperone.

On the day of the show, I'm informed that people may stand up during the performance. I inquisitively ask why when it's seated—no chairs as far as I could see have been taken out.
"It depends on whether people choose to dance or not!"
But I'm placed behind these people so how will I see?
I'm abruptly informed, *"that's the problem with wheelchairs!"*
So now it is my wheelchair's fault that a) I can't see and b) my wheelchair cannot stand up!
If only they considered how ridiculous they sounded.
There's certainly no consideration for me in all this and my wheelchair is treated like a worthless apprentice.

Heavyweight doors,
recently mopped floors,

poorly lit lamps, too steep ramps,
other theatre users (who decide to dance).
Why is everything too high or too low?
It's not my brain that is disabled, it's other people's perception.
They should try using a wheelchair,
to discover what boundaries are already made,
solutions need to be considered rather than appointing blame.

Who Do I Wake Up As?

I am the sun and rain
amongst the rainbows again.
I'm flying solo;
my mind the parachute.
Flying high but free-falling too.
This is not my personality
lugged around in this suitcase.

Without measuring my sleep,
life is lived in narrow margins.
Buzzing one minute; short-circuited next.
I never know what version of me I will wake up to be,
as my mind simply evaporates.
I do not mean to wound those I care for
when flames rise and water drowns.

My heart is banging on chest's door.
At times its painful like cuts and burns.
I'm a Rubix Cube with all its twists and turns.
Angels show me visions of my death
if I don't conform to their orders.
Orders that were once expectations.
I'm falling and failing again.

The Chameleon Salute

Good morning! Good morning!
I open my eyes, yet I'm still exhausted.
I lay in bed awake and think about the day ahead.
'What can I be thankful for?'
—a list recited five times.

I have a place to call home.
I don't owe anybody any money.
I have family and friends around me.
I have my own independence.
I enjoy making and creating art.

I have a place to call home.
I don't owe anybody any money.
I have family and friends around me.
I have my own independence.
I enjoy making and creating art.

I have a place to call home.
I don't owe anybody any money.
I have family and friends around me.
I have my own independence.
I enjoy making and creating art.

I have a place to call home.
I don't owe anybody any money.
I have family and friends around me.
I have my own independence.
I enjoy making and creating art.

I have a place to call home.
I don't owe anybody any money.
I have family and friends around me.
I have my own independence.
I enjoy making and creating art.

Yet, I struggle to see beyond the brain fog;
my sleep-wake cycle has gone to pot,
as I consider what I need to get up for: NOT;
a shower, get dressed, a cup of tea;
all tasks that mean nothing to me.
I need to take 'gratitude on the go'
swing my mood out the window.

But, I have no energy,
I'm riddled with lethargy.
However, it's strategy I seek,
every minute, every hour, every day, every week.
Motivation and drive,
two words—thin veins
to keep me alive.
I struggle with both
with a lack of interest in anything to boast.

Bring to position,
get out of my lazy bed.
Posture: I stretch out those morning blues.
No hunching: check in the mirror.
An inch above the right eye transfixed.
Straight back and digits tightly locked.
Intimidation felt.
Hormones amped.
Head locked ready to launch;
remaining eye contact at all times.
Arm elevates in one crisp movement
in line with my shoulder
and I salute you.
I salute you out of respect
and camaraderie.
Not because I'm inferior
I affirm 'I salute you'
before I stand down
which is completed like symmetry.

I salute you.
I salute you.
I salute you.
I salute you.
I salute you.

Back and Forth

I'm so busy ignoring my feelings,
it's the only way to cope.
All I wish for is my racing heart to tell
my heavy heart that there is hope.

Distractions cause disassociation.
My coping mechanism for staying busy.
Sat on my hands fearing retaliation,
quantified risks, making me dizzy.

I've written more poems this week
than I managed in the previous six.
Taken a diploma to improve my technique—
my prose lifts my mood like a rising phoenix.

But what other options do I have?
Medication increases the pendulum swing;
no concept of time or place, like an outdated sat-nav
my eyes weep and tears sting.

My psychic phoenix reveals her vulnerability,
disturbed patterns of thinking;
a desired blend of sobriety.
Something needs to stop the sinking now.

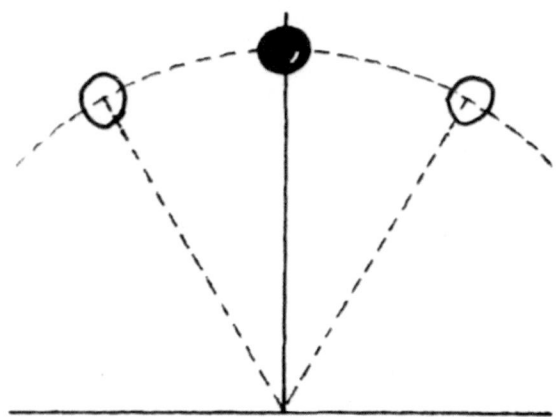

What My Body Needs Most

I'm in pain
and you're not giving me what I need.
I know my body,
I know what it needs.
It needs YOU to understand MY pain!
I'm not easily relieved,
my body smarting;
troubled, tortured and tormented.
It's agonising and unbearable.
Those hard-hitting drugs missing the mark.

This crippling affliction bears misery and distress,
sufferance, heartbreak, anguish, unhappiness.
What I need is pain management
because I can't do this myself!
I need you on board to support me and my health.
I am haunted with pain every single day,
where we share each other's bodies,
set the bar and just pray.
Pain should only be tolerated
in return for living day-to-day life,
but there's always a price to pay.
There's no paradise!

I lose control and It makes demands I cannot meet,
'cos you just don't understand what my body needs most.
I have a limit.
I'll take what you give.
I ask for more.
I have to wait.
THE PAIN isn't going away.
I ask again, and again and again.
You tell me there's no more,
but I need more.

THE PAIN isn't like any other.
It's squeezing my insides out,
spasms richer than gold.
It's rebellious energy, rapturous eruptions and
raging explosions hurting so bad,
repeating one after another.

Nerves revolt in an act of protest.
My body cries out.
The extra pain relief delivered at last—
painkiller,
pain reliever,
narcotics, I just don't care!
Worries absorbed,
future intended,
a life better now than the one recommended.

My Autumn Dungarees

Autumn wears stone denim dungarees,
with patches of mushrooms covering its knees.
Dried leaves fall from hawthorn hedges and hems,
revealing worm-wriggling stitches, disguised hidden gems.
It's in need of support, like saddleless shorts,
shining needles of rain to bring new life once again.
Fretful and fruitless blown,
cyclones of energy lower the tone.
In exchange for its summer flip-flops,
appear the mossy woollen snug socks.
Where trunky legs even adorn warmer sheepskin boots,
as the once flowering fantasia returns to its roots.
A patterned life where slim clouds once sang,
and an indulgence of lavender ready to hang.
Autumn is a time for recovery.
A new voyage, a new coat, desperate for discovery.

Biscuit Tin

Biscuit tin—empty
Taste diminished in crumbs left
Waiting my new fill.

Feeling the Frost

(In response to listening to Vivaldi 'Winter')

Frost draped around me.
Winter is here.
Two pairs of socks, an extra layer.
A warm flask of home-made chicken soup.
I carefully consider what else to wear.
If only my clothing had a warming feature.
Where feathers were ignited,
foam filling plugged in,
fleece free from feeling the chill.
Warmth maintained on the go.

Frost draped around me.
Nature is asleep.
Metabolism depressed coma-like;
they call it hibernation.
Completely immobile,
frozen below freezing
the consumption of energy to heat itself nullified.
Hedgehogs, bats, dormouse, rodents, badgers and bees.
If only taking a nap was that easy!

Frost draped upon me.
Nature is still asleep!
An anxiety of snowdrops appears,
whilst the carpets of bluebells are still hiding,
waiting patiently for springtime.
Our woodlands would soon be transformed,
but only for a short while
because the canopy will close up.
New leaves blocking sunlight.

Simply 'Because'
A butterfly cinquain

Because
Black Lives Matter
Illustrates injustice
Power in black identity
One world
Colonisation cast shadows
Brushed under the carpet
Black people fought
Traced shapes

Leaving by the Back Door

It was that dim dark hour when things just crept out of darkness.
Bushes still inky black, the sky colourless and cheerless,
clouds like a tor veil.
The sun wore a dim pale eye, behind a socket of grey haze.

I'd gone out through the back door, shrewdly trampling over shadows.
I'd left an empty gaping window frame, broken panes and unloved paint,
a door without a lock, a knocker or a handle!
A sorry state of a building left in the rear.

Next to the high stone wall lay a sinister hedge of prickly, tangled branches,
choking the weeds and strangling the path.
The grass was withered and brown, plastic bags instead of blossoms
flapped in the bushes, spewing their contents on the ground.

At the side of the door was a pile of stones—the only company as the
letterbox moans—
a shattered wall, pitted as if gnawed by hundreds of starving rats.
On its back a crumbling chimney stack.

And the hanging foul-mouthed gutter was clogged with rotting leaves.
No intention to pardon the grieving trees.
It's all in a sorry state as I approach the unhinged fragile gate,
contemplating leaving by the front door if it's not too late.

As the sun's merciless heat beats down like an invisible hammer,
nature was painting the hills.
The sky was flawlessly blue without a tinge or a hue.
It promises to be the canvas for laughter and the home for life ever after.

I sat still in the arched wooden porchway where staring back at me were the beautiful
carved white shutters;
my built-in cosy peaceful haven; perfect in every way,
even down to how the flowerbeds lay.

The garden bathes in dawn's first illuminating rays;
vivid, sparkling treasures—welcome spring days.
A symphony of songbirds ride in the wind,
through the empty branches, slightly skinned.

Poppies and daisies wave like hundreds of hands.
Some lay like confetti across Mediterranean sands.
Welcome wave by wave are the nodding gent's heads of lilac,
forming a patchwork pillow of beauty; upright colours called to duty.

The paintwork is fresh, tidy and chic.
The garden furniture is consummate, resplendently stained in teak.
The front door is open like baptism to passions gate; where soprano
thrushes tend to mate,
where quivering chaffinch pick through harvest, recognising those elegant suavests.

It's like living two totally different lives.
Just imagine if we were asked to swap sides!
Imagine if the vivid blue sky is layered with pregnant clouds;
the whispers would not be far behind!
Imagine if the birds suddenly stopped singing.
Would you lie if all of a sudden if turned grey?
Could we have a life using both doors?
Treading the sentiment of each other's floors.
Maybe exchange some of what was one way for another;
so after all the only difference is 'Mother'.

Hairdryer in the City

I was once asked, "Do you ever hear strange sounds coming from that machine and wonder if it's trying to tell you something?" We are now in a landscape where more electric vehicles take to the road compared to times past when nothing was remotely electric and we had a bad habit of running out of fuel!

I hear distinctive coughing;
from what my daughter describes as 'a hairdryer on wheels!'
I can hear a chorus of engines revving and roaring.
Vroom! Vroom! Vroom!
Revolutions of energy as the green light appears.
Vroom! Vroom! Vroom!
It's gurgling,
spluttering and spewing;
to the point of almost choking as it exits the STOP sign,
then propels itself forward again on green,
like a coiled spring.
On its transition through amber,
it rumbles and reverberates,
thunders when the accelerator engages;
babbles and ripples.
As the next set of lights are approached,
The sincerity of the brakes are applied.
It rattles and squeaks;
as you apply pressure
to slow down;
purling through the gears,
to slooowww down.
Whining and vibrating as it sits on red;
a chance to cool down,
yet nothing is said.
Hissing! Hissing!
awaiting the next light,
Hissing! Hissing!
The mechanics inside the inductive loop.
Now amber is here, it offers a contingency plan,
whereas green instructs us to move along.
Time spent on red and green is equal,
yet time spent on amber seems brief.
We do get two chances to 'get ready'
Twice vrooming and hissing ready to change.
Non-verbal and optical communication switched on.

Transition

This is my warning to you,
as I open my mouth,
puff out my chest
and raise my front legs.

I'm feeling threatened.
I'm hot and need to cool off.
I am struggling to breathe.
I am emotionally stressed.

I was content in the cage,
until you put in your hand.
I panicked and clung to the walls,
breaching barriers opened doors.

It's a survival instinct,
from a learned experience.
Fear is replaced by impatience.
Transition gradual and patient.

No conception of affection,
yet a sense of security I demand.
All my life I've feared rejection,
from your own intrusive hands.

I'm swaying on my hind legs,
so I can bite in any direction.
Emotions should be 'worn on a sleeve';
as memories need time to grieve.
With my body now compressed,
in a mix of colours I'm dressed.
I'm ready to move forward,
just bear in mind—changing places isn't straight-forward.

Toxicity

I'm awakened
by song-filled, open-throated birds,
in the milk-white summer sky,
underneath a lawn of blessed crocuses;
as God's paintbrush sweeps across
a green palette, with hues of brown and yellow.

The sweet smell of freshly cut grass tickles my nostrils,
my eyes electrocuted and my mouth scratched;
hay-fever boiling my emotions.
Purple and orange splatters, follow the pace of life,
stray patches of grey dip and dinner in the distance,
where air hatches an occasional joke.

My mood sits on the fence,
rent remains unpaid—colourless,
lacking distinctive character or interest,
even the cellar unable to drag itself upstairs,
to share in the practicalities of life;
and relieve toxic debt.

Whilst my heart palpitates,
pounding and thumping ectopically
I refrain from 'my poison'
and consider colour in a rainbow no longer tarnished,
and wipe chunks of charcoal from my lips.
I am very much awake now.

My Brain is a Compass

Facing North, I'm excited about future events.
I'm happy, with a good sense of well-being.
I'm very focused and determined to complete tasks.
I'm arranging events that will bring immediate success.

But then I look South where I'm irritable and easily agitated.
I'm hearing voices and sense that I'm being followed.
I'm anxious and loaded with horrible thoughts—
I'm failing in all this,
depressed, considering my value to others.

To the East, I'm easily distracted
my thoughts race against each other
and I can't concentrate.
Now, what was it I needed to say?
There's a constant battle
between looking left or right.

To the West, I'm adventurous and confident.
I'm untouchable as I perform angelically.
I can achieve anything if I put my mind to it.
I feel invincible too.
I don't need to sleep.
I'm over-friendly to others.

Apparently, I'm doing things that are ridiculous,
like weeding council
footpaths!
I've taken risks with my meds and
laboured cuttings to reduce the pain.
It takes time transitioning between North, East, South and West,
adjusting the way I face and who I turn my back on.
In between North East/North West and South East/South West
I'm able to cope with a balanced approach.
I start to feel happier
However, it might look like I don't know where I'm going,
but that's the way I like it!
My brain creates its own journey and my heart another.

Compensatory Bandages

I ask myself the question: How could something bad (mental illness) lead to something good (creativity)?

Good is bad
Bad is good
Creativity is good
Mood is bad
All my malfunctions get weeded out over time.

Affection and cognition
Affection and creativity
Order and disorder
Flying high and low
The road ahead.

Mixed mood and dual thoughts
Problem perception
Mood and solution
Mood and strategy
Mood swings

Bipolarity, ambivalence and creative thinking
The bright side of being blue
Influence and decisions
Emotion induction
Cognition and emotion

Art Therapy
Inspiration and the creative process
Conceptions of colours
Conceptions of mental illness
Creativity in compensatory bandages

Studies of people, creative people
Biological and genetics
The bigger picture
All kinds of geniuses
Creative and literary geniuses

Behaviour
Personality traits
ADHD, Schizophrenia to name only two
Degrees of Top-Down Control
on information processing temperament

Benefits of laughter
Benefits of humour
Music therapy
Other artistic pursuits—
ruminating.

You simply can't put a plaster on it
Soothe it with ice or heat
Wrap a bandage around fear
But what you can do—
is listen.

A Little Bit of Me...

I need to fall in love with myself,
have confidence no matter what,
to let my mind and body rest,
and to stop paddling blind;
determine the values I am proud of
and embrace my strengths.
I need to unconsciously adopt limiting beliefs
and find empowering ones instead.

and a little bit more...

I need to change perspective,
openly practice self-love,
create healthy routines,
and put the boat back on buoyant waters;
unlock the power of proximity and
face my fears.
I need to change my focus
and take credit for my achievements.

with a few extras too.

I need to trust
and accept what is true,
have faith in my actions,
make quick fix repairs;
stop blaming myself and
know those challenging times will pass.
I need to be who I am
and recall that life is a gift.

Advice from a Pencil on How to Diet

Look at my slim, slender figure;
all in one form with no bumps or curves.
You use me to stir your low-fat milkshake
before wiping your Weight Watcher logo clean.
I'm a colourful sort,
with delicate lines around my waist.
Between finger and thumb, you pick me up,
just as you 'wood' to eat,
except I'm an eco-friendly sort.
I'm made to last, whilst you continue to fast.
You put obstacles in your way,
only glancing through recipes,
you're not in the mood for the right kind of food.
You lack the willpower to lose any weight
and allow the looks of others to frustrate.
Fill your plate with plenty of veg,
park all those sugars on the edge.
Negotiate choices of lean meat
and check products for excessive wheat.
Drinking is fine, just one glass of wine;
or stick with water or modified no-sugar flavourings.
You need to exercise and stay active,
count steps, staying physically reactive.
All you need to do now is take note,
sharpen your pencil and revisit what I've wrote.

Still — Who? What? Where? Why? When? The Teacher Asked.

My (Who?) heart beats empty hope (What?)
Where? Why? and When?
I can only reflect on life and where it is heading (Where?),
If it is still (Why?)
I can look at flowers, trees, squirrels and clouds.
When I am still (When?)
What could be more pure than a white rose?
If I embrace stillness.
I can take nourishment
in who I am not but who I am meant to be.
Only when I am still,
and solitary
can I teach without fear,
distinguish positives and negatives,
believe in power and courage;
as without it, I am frozen and afraid.

When I practise stillness,
I must stop blaming myself and others,
for only I can truly perceive more or less.
I must do away with excess baggage,
strip out those thorns,
and clearly, question who I am;
recall that life is a gift,
trust,
heed faith,
take confidence,
And fall back in love with myself.

Then I can embrace strengths and weaknesses equally
because I am still—
I can distinguish between something that exists and
something that is true,
purity embraced, during stillness.
I am still—
With freedom from noise,
hushed silence,
quiescent,
still.

Life is a Tapestry

I was five, six, seven, eight,
when I knew I wasn't 'straight'.
I was confused, young and whatever I tried,
one male, one female—two powers preside.
Parents simply told me *'Learn to love yourself on the inside as much as your outside'*.

I didn't want to look pretty, I yearned to be strong
BUT afraid to look in the mirror.
I felt a reflection breathing down my neck,
salty tears in my tissue;
when bravery was all that I needed to pick.
People would judge and mock.
I'm not a freak or weak.
I'd simply sown unique stitches in my own tapestry.
Curiosity over-sexualised.
It's up to others to accept or reject!

When you first look at me,
what do you see?
I'd stolen years in silence,
plagued by questions.
Two people sharing one body.
I'd asked Jesus to fix me.
I'd swallowed insults and slurs.
I was a naked question,
yet dressed up to answer.
I would hide until I could face
who I wanted to see,
walking between worlds.
How do I relate to my own body?
Poetry – my lens of possibility.

A mismatch between biological sex and gender identity.
I'd bind my chest to avoid telltale signs of my sex,
withdrawn and socially isolated,
low self-esteem.
I'd change my name and pronouns,
paralysed with fear constantly.
I had no language to explain what happened
when depressive episodes started.
I wanted to punch the mirror.
Trying to repress and change gender identity didn't work.
Spent years feeling I didn't fit in.
To begin gender transition takes a lot of reflection
It must feel normal and right to begin.

When will I match my outer shell with its inner truth?
I knew something was still not right
and it had felt that way for a long time.
I'm a female one day and a male the next.
It's much more bewildering than that.
The level of discomfort in my body
needs to change,
constant reminders that my body
and mind are not in sync.
Prejudice.
Conversation feels too difficult.

Scared

Poetic Emancipation

In the creation of poetry—
the heart
and mind must be readied.
The emotional and mental preparation
waiting
there to be steaded.
It is an act
of imagination,
in the moment
of certainty,
where words
        musically ebb and flow
                      creating poetic emancipation.

ALONE

Living by my authentic self,
I am ALONE.
Expectations,
shame and judgement.
In a room full of mirrors,
each opinion adds a layer of dust.
Do I smash the mirrors?
Look at the blurry image
or roll up my sleeves
and begin wiping the dust away.
I was born myself.
Nothing more—nothing less.
Taking my first steps,
I interacted with others.
No compass.
Too young for philosophical thought.
Expectations were set not taught.
How I should / shouldn't be.
Parents, friends, boss and strangers.
Now it's all about responsibility.
If I live life my way,
(when others may not agree),
I simply 'LIVE IT'
Even if judged,
I live without fearing
no one will love me.
If I live life as my entire self.
I will not be ALONE.

Darkened Space

I have no photo albums of my childhood—
no story of which to speak of
because not being believed is salt in the wounds.
I wish I could have escaped
but being locked away inside was the norm.
I'd disappear before dark
and awake after dark;
awaiting the key to turn in the lock,
the door to open and
whereupon I'd await further instruction.

There was minimal space to move.
A small low-level shelf next to a set of cupboards
served as a place to dangle my legs.
It was quiet and solitary; cold at times too.
With nobody to communicate with
I was left to talk to myself.
I spent hours considering how to get
out and record my thoughts on paper,
however, my cell was bare
and bereft of daylight.

One day I stole a pen-torch
and hid it amongst my jumpers.
Petty theft was my thing!
It took me weeks to get a notebook
small enough to also hide
and what felt like forever to
bring a writing implement to my abode.
If I could record my fears on paper
maybe there was a chance
that somebody would believe me.

Reassured being inside was for my own good
I struggled to see how sleeping upright
was best as my bed lay bare.
I started to make a list
of possible reasons why
they kept hold of the key.
It wasn't even as if I was any trouble.
What was it I'd done that put me away?
Forbidden to talk, I held my tongue
and started to write.

I recorded my fears in indelible ink,
marks that could not be erased.
Blood-stained items spoke volumes
when removed supposedly for me to wear.
I began forming tattoos that couldn't be found
but hurt as I forced the nib beneath my skin
Symbols of hidden meanings
personal to me,
yet prominent, jabbed entries that scar.
Messages distorted as scribed too deep.

For how many days, months or even years
did I serve,
before being locked up was no more?
Had I simply just outgrown the space,
or did the place hold a different purpose?
Was I old enough? Was I better behaved?
What was the reason without the ability to ask?
I would never find out, so made one simple assumption—
The wardrobe was too small
and the shed became the grown-up version.

Medium-sized

I am a hungry, colourful caterpillar with very distinctive lippy,
where each segment of me wears its own trousers
and shoes contrast with matching socks.
I'm blinded with the benefit of superior vision,
although conned into believing I have more power
in my legs than I really do.
My head is awash with poppy seeds,
who vandalise my emotions and separate thought,
who fail to take on responsibility.
I'm left to wax and wane like an ecliptic moon,
where fine threads of energy give me purpose,
studded pockets carry supplies in my khaki jeans,
all of which is camouflage suited size medium.
I am a majestic fairground, turning me upside down and inside out,
like huge flapping tarpaulin sheets injected with lights,
where screams linger from the bigger rides.
Amongst muddied walkways that are all but guides—
not suitable for my chair who cannot walk,
nor legs who stop to talk.
not forgetting the bag I carry,
that in itself if medium-sized
And who laughs one minute and cries the next.

The Indigo Starseed

I'm an angel
Though not a successful one yet?
I'm an angel
An Indigo Starseed? Not yet?
Earth is the playground for my soul
Aware of feelings—unscripted my goal
To awaken people out of darkness
To bring new ideas
I'm just a practising Earth angel in flight
Anchoring the timeline of peace, love and light

I'm special, out of this world;
pushing boundaries utterly absurd.
A new state of consciousness I take thee,
whilst my body transmits an indigo aura in me.
A calling to make the world a better place.
A feeling of natural superiority I trace.
Innate knowledge of how to do things
Love for nature, humanity—all beings.
I'm an angel.
Though not a successful one yet!

I'm called by the soul to help others.
No interest in money just life as it gathers.
Intuitive, strong-willed—my sensitivity weathers;
I'm here for a reason—fairness, just living pothers.
Sensitive in both a physical/emotional sense;
thinking in terms of possibility, potential and resilience.
Whilst I'm not great at setting the boundaries evidenced.
I'm an Indigo Starseed—my inheritance.
I'm an angel.

My Social Chameleon

I shift my hues whilst contemplating my movement across new branches.
I'm a plethora of colour as my tongue propels like a fighter jet.
I play truth or dare amongst the shadows of silhouettes.
I wait patiently for the green light before following my fancies.
I rotate on my branch to nip the unsuspecting bug;
my helmet tethered with binocular vision.
I have the advantage against predators,
hunting with my eyes wide open.
I shower in a plant pot with my keeper
Heated emissions of light bounce off my back
displaying anger and militancy in my pack.
I am still alive with a name,
along with likes, dislikes and shortcomings.
I'm not that different to a chameleon really
I'm a colourful character with spritely moves.
It's very hard to explain the overwhelming power
and to forget what's in my head
and to focus upon what I've done and said.
I only wear a helmet if I need to.
And am happy to shower on my own, providing
I can repeat this over and over again.
Hiding is counterproductive,
I need to show my true colours.
I know people look at me and want answers
But OCD isn't something you broadcast.
I'm simply Earth's lion influenced by mood;
my Social Chameleon.

It Smelt of Love

I wonder what it smells like to be the King.
I doubt he's as tasteful as a Kentucky Fried Chicken wing!
Tastes that accompany smells, both deep to the core.
That 'older' people smell.
The smell of the outdoors.
We can smell our own fear and despair.
Memories of affection that fit together
like old wooden children's jigsaws.
Smells ranked and stank without a clothes peg.
Aroma defined as an odour,
in the back of your mouth—
minty, chemical, fruity or plain pungent.
Fragrant flowers smell of love
for a birthday, a 'Thank You', or an anniversary,
a new home, good luck and one out of sympathy.
Cherish the gift to smell.
I wonder what I smell like.

Colours — Which One Am I Today?

I am Green—on the verge of creation,
amongst sensitive echoes along nature's complexion.
An inner voice drives motivation
that actuates the mind.
As I look left I am orange.
A poet full of optimistic juices
generous in her sharing.
If I could shed schedules,
in favour of spontaneity,
would my freedom be at risk?
As I look right I am white,
not yet complete, pure or whole,
I am new—neat and
well-balanced.
If I look ahead I hope to see a rainbow;
a visible spectrum with the highest vibrations,
interchangeable colours of strength
I am a colour,
a union of body and soul,
no end to my visual pollution,
yet still vulnerable
to judgement on any wavelength.

What Can 'Red' Do?

Red **a**pplauds love.
Red **b**links to free dust.
Red **c**hokes on toast.
Red **d**elivers a dove.

Red **e**ducates North American Indians.
Red **f**rightens blue.
Red **g**uides the arrows.
Red **h**unts Darwinians and howls out at dawn.

Red **i**nvites infection.
Red **j**uggles pepperoni.
Red **k**neels on the lawn.
Red **l**anguishes in prison.

Red **m**easures the ruler.
Red **n**otices the time.
Red **o**pens snake eyes.
Red **p**olices prowlers.

Red **q**uantifies linguistic elements.
Red **r**educes cholesterol.
Red **s**educes the sun.
Red **t**eases the gin bottle.

Red **u**ndresses Jelly Babies.
Red **v**alues suncream.
Red **w**restles radish.
Red **x**enon is distilled.
Red **y**awns contagiously, as
Red **z**igzags through the alphabet.

One Hundred Years Ago...

Tutankhamun was toxic.
Orpiment pigment and arsenic
imperishable and indestructible.
His parentage was relatively unknown.
Yet an ancient god—all skin and bone.

Discovered one hundred years ago amongst much propaganda
was a three-piece tomb, heavier than a giant panda.
Behind a dismantled doorway in a yellow-carpeted room,
he lay in this nondescript, borrowed tomb.
It was nothing like his labyrinth neighbours!

Hieroglyphics hushed.
Voiceless emotions crushed.
His legacy lost in sands of time.
His death, an end to bloodline.
'Wonderful things' to be found.

He'd wore orthopaedic sandals,
held onto over a hundred walking stick handles.
His name stricken from the 'Kings List',
monuments usurped, listed a fatalist.
Five thousand priceless treasures.

...hidden by debris;
was treasure decorated with gold leaf.
Entry had been plundered to the forgotten location;
other tombs built on top.
Gold in abundance.

For Which Environment?

A powerful accent of colour—
formal,
solemn,
heavy.
It's dignified tuxedo,
shielding negative energy.
Black magic.
Unspoken engineering.
Intimidating, marvelling back into authority.

An aura of suspicion—
polished, shadowed,
misunderstood.
Amongst unattended shade.
Acoustics beyond the mountain range.
Mystery.
Liquorice wheels,
transformed, handed out like dominoes.

Its breath is a reflex—fertile,
a melody,
running
through its blackened heart,
yet elegance is eroded.
Grounded,
energised thoughts.
In any environment simply BLACK.

My Awkward Aura

As I lie on the treatment plinth
he works around me and above me,
sending intentions of colour towards me:
Willing them into my body.
I bathe in colour,
palettes of seasonal colour.
An atmosphere full or aroma,
mystique and illusion set free.
My awkward aura wears a halo
that gives way to my ambient karma,
whilst all notions of romance rid,
overtones tempered and semblance slid.

Old Oak Tree

She fell from an old oak tree,
like wild food foraged sustainably,
desperate to find presence;
strength in her identity.
She underestimated resiliency
but began to talk frank—openly,
so…that was testimony.

As she grew older by age
she became more valuable,
and craved
developing cavities,
crevices, dead wood and other features;
like an old oak tree
whose foliage and nature she adorned.
The perfect haven and support.

Can You Erase the Future?

I pencil in an outline of the future.
Graphite markings of no particular size or shape;
conscious to leave something only barely visible,
yet held down securely by masking tape.

The image has an effortless shadow.
Disguised by tired cross-hatched shading,
purposely neglecting the criminal links,
Justice serves time on those creamy pastel pinks.

An image I clearly remember,
from that late evening twenty years last September.
My memory serves me a lingering purpose,
germs ruminating on the infectious surface.

It may be too late for that someone;
an image I can barely forebear.
Fearing judgement in my own sketching,
yet a lifetime I'd shared.

With no right or wrong on paper.
With the absence of definitive words.
I can erase the past very easily—on paper.
But not in my mind—
ridiculous,
farcical
utterly, absurd!

The Difference Amongst Moons

Skies were alive…
…as the Sturgeon Moon rose
on Thursday capturing all in its glory.
It's the closest we've been for a while;
as summer slips away into autumn
and nights begin to grow longer.
The Sturgeon Moon emanates its presence;
Earth and Moon align.

Reaching its Zenith on Friday
morning has never been this big before.
Hues of colour sharpened around the globe,
I'm now at the highest point reached in the heavens,
at a position that will not change;
a plumb line denotes its accuracy.
Moon and Earth align.

With gratitude for nature's celestial beauty,
we blame you for sleepless nights.
We ruminate on your delivery
like a newborn baby sparing the silence.
Your disruption asks us to step forward;
hormones on ice
as you both align.

Changing Places

Changes—hit replay.
Reverse the changes,
recharge and play.
Narrow minds bleeding;
speeding through.
Racing changes
places, people
 pictures, painted.
Silence depicted,
images muted.
Replay the changes,
reverse all play.
If it's not necessary,
don't recharge today.

Alien Brand

I'm tempted to try an alien brand
but I won't (can't) let my daughter know firsthand.
She doesn't like change;
especially when new means 'strange'
I replace the contents of one bottle with another,
putting the lid on the remains of the other;
wondering whether she will even notice.
The colour is clearly different if nothing else

I expect *"Why is this 'Comfort' not blue anymore?"*
The colour is clearly different to that before.
"When did it change?"
I answer with "It is just a re-brand, like a 'part-exchange'."
Not realising she was in the cupboard staring at the alternative.
I conceded the change but justified the motive.
We could have twice as much and the fragrance was nice,
notwithstanding the reduction in price.
I offered a washing amnesty and peaceful boycott,
unsure whether I had won that battle or not.
She'd be in a state, feeling exasperate,
so I continued to let my mum do her washing separate.

Pretending

I'm a social chameleon,
blending into an environment of change,
where time has no presence;
emptiness marked on the range.
Where is my identity in all this?
I am abandoned by risk,
I wear pain in my reflection,
dive head first into a tailspin,
estranged by communication.
My void hollowed-out in ink.
I simply do not care what others think.

It hurts to pretend
to keep on pretending;
then pretend some more.
My heart's makeshift scaffolding
is articulate like a spider's web.
I'm invalidated, I'm pervasive.
And it hurts to keep on pretending.
What excuse can I now give?
Mixed-up feedback challenged
so I pretend.
Pretend.
Pretend to hush my crying.
Pretend to enjoy the empty space.
Emptiness suppressed.
Emptiness challenged;
vulnerable to life's vagaries.
The total sum of me
transparent, versatile, mimicked.
Unconsciously pretending—
I pretend some more.
Pretending.
I pretend.

Cargo
(An Adelaide Crapsey Cinquian)

Black lives
Sold in cargo
Like cattle in labour
Brutal transatlantic voyage
Enslaved

Fighting
Identity
Colonised Africa
Whites join in—abolition now
oppressed

The Raceless Race

I woke up white
in a black world.
I wasn't a racist
I was a good person
but colour was much misunderstood.

I didn't think I had a race
race was for brown/black-skinned people.
I thought white
was the raceless race,
Colours misunderstood.

I thought culture and ethnicity
were for people of other races,
and from other countries.
I silently struggled with race.
Colours misunderstood.

I wanted friends of colour
but always attracted white friends.
When I was with a person of colour
I felt tense and feared saying something offensive.
Colours misunderstood.

Being white felt invisible.
White was the default.
Whiteness was the absence of race,
yet structures our lives.
Race being socially structured
Racial hierarchy put whites at the top;
not the product of nature,
but of society.
Black people were the indigenous people
and all other people of colour were lesser.

Empty Echoes

As echoes creep along my tongue
they become scared.
As colours kiss
they infuse emotion.
As silhouettes lie down
their halos reflect.
As my image is mirrored
echoes suddenly stop.

Born into a New Form

I am borderline grey.
I have no fancies or frills.
I stand naked on the stone windowsill,
detached from my holder.
I've had my sheets whipped off
contemplating my 'end'.
Earlier this week I was fully loaded,
ready to discharge, bitter and eroded.

Children used to dress me,
seasonal snowmen to spring scarecrows,
creativity in young hands.
BUT apparently, I'm a concern; withstands
lingering contamination that might even kill;
health and safety gone mad.

I'd like to think I could be an ornament (nothing posh)
BUT unless hands forget about me
I could stand here for days without a wash!
I look out of place, awkward and insecure,
fearing the wire basket, when
cleaning day will see me replaced.

I'm a comedian at heart,
my personality dry and priceless.
Aloe vera fragrants my core,
an imprint arresting my torso.
Now the empty and bare awkwardness survives
having served my purpose.

How long will I wait?
What constitutes my fate?
I sit neither the right way up or upside down,
an autumn breeze tickling my spine as I wait.
Hopefully, I won't get the chance to be lonely,
knowing fellow Kellogg's and Kipling
are already mingling in the blue bin,
later to be recycled in a different form.
It's here that a new life will be born.

                Thank you from 'The Toilet Roll Holder'

The Sum of Me!

A little bit of quietness brings me gratitude;
a fleeting moment of inner peace and stillness.
Like a sponge, I soak in the silence
and follow the example of tranquillity.

I prioritise and focus to keep my mind refreshed,
remain calm, serene, in control of myself,
unplug any technology and go back to basics.
I draw, paint, crochet—I'm creatively free.

I embrace the stillness within my grasp,
whether I sing in private or simply dance along.
As I wander amongst trees my spirit lifts;
the healing powers to be at one with nature.

If I'm tempted to veer towards an unhealthy diet,
I cut back on consumption and change preparation—
a fulfilling breakfast, lunch or dinner to enjoy;
add rituals with time to savour the flavours.

Having the right mindset before you go about your day
is like giving your garden a facelift, yet dressed clumsily.
It's time to change clutter for space, in which to decorate.
You cannot see the most beautiful things in the world,
but you can touch them; silence is a luxury.

I made the choice when seeking sacred space,
away from the chores in day-to-day life.
Enjoy that single minute alone; give yourself a chance,
acknowledge the neglected parts, appreciate creating yourself.

Silence hides inside as I grapple for productivity,
feeling capable and notice small successes.
Quiet moments open doors for great experiences.
Calmness comes with relaxed routine rest.

I struggle to acknowledge when enough is enough.
When my efforts are undervalued I get equally stressed.
I need to say 'No' and be happy with my answer,
without feeling I'm letting down others in addition to me.

Whatever makes us happy, we should do more of,
detox negative energy, take action and move on,
make the most of productivity, bring energy to life,
and don't be afraid to ask, rescue with favours, learn to rest.

I turn problems into possibilities by opening the door—
to listen, reflect, to walk new pathways, to recognise.
I don't need to explain that I am enough.
My brain thrives on empty stimulation, quiet by choice,
yet I never get past four in my countdown tricks.

A little less perfection would take the pressure off,
accept mistakes happen and just get things done.
I must have a laugh even if things go wrong;
if I'm unsatisfied I seek positive change—
for this is the sum of me.

Simply Anything

What is rain without any soul?
What is loneliness like in a crowd?
What is a crossword without any clues?
What is the moon without a tattoo?
What is solitude without a wilderness?
What is comfort without a teddy bear?
What is imagination with a brain overload?
What is a mask worn back to front?
What is praise never mentioned or recorded?
What is an audience without the main act?
What is progress without no starting point?
What is a clock without any hands?
What is a secret without energy and warmth?
What are pebbles without water?
What is a mirror hung back to front?
What is laughter without a comedian or a smile?
What is comparable to the value of life?
What Ian anything that could be something else?
What if that something is simply anything?

Canary Girls

I was on my feet
hours upon hours,
only short breaks allowed.
Seven days straight, week after week
only occasional leave granted.
Faced with the ever-present threat of an explosion.

Women conscripted without any training,
hot TNT was poured from the huge vat
into the heavy shells.
No form of protection.
Detonators inserted too.
Carefully,
I'd scrape the toxic waste level
with my bare hands.
Carefully,
I'd ensure I didn't trigger
a charge to blow up the bullet.
Atmosphere tense.

No hair grips permitted and
only wireless bras to be worn.
No silk scarfs or
nylon slacks;
avoiding creating static
to detonate the charge.
I'd already seen munitionettes ignite a shell,
injuring fellow workers, it was hell.
A metallic taste lingered in my mouth.

The risk of amputation
passed through my hands every day.
The loss of fingers and thumbs,
burns and blindness per se.
Devils porridge leaving scars.
Cosmetic consequences a given.
All for two-thirds of a soldier's pay.

Skin yellowed from the toxic TNT
like the plumage of a canary.
Hair a shade of green like a glass bottle
or ginger like malt vinegar.
Its poison caused anaemia and jaundice,
despite milk offered to combat the effects.
Canary Babies delivered a yellow hue too.

Factories were unable to meet the government demands
as the production of munitions increased,
taking our loved ones to the front
and depleting the male workforces.
They didn't give us credit,
unsure we were capable,
when in fact they worried
that returning workers couldn't be employed.
Discolouration faded with time.

My History...

My history is made up of empty prompts that attest to my resilience.

- the location of my history stems down to the coal face
- the instrument of my history was silenced drums
- the complications of my history are awakened amid flashing blue lights
- the tribulation of my history had me immobilised by mistake
- the colour of my history was and is anything tinged purple
- the triumph of my history was publication
- the looks of my history are locked tightly away
- the trials of my history can be unpicked with a blunt needle
- the secret of my history was sharing affliction
- the sound of my history was 'Kerplunk'
- the music of my history was paused in the Autumn of Four Seasons by Vivaldi
- the celebration of my history was over 30 years of marriage
- the taste of my history was over-sweetened tea in a plastic cup
- the people of my history remain unforgiven
- the food of my history was a family meatloaf
- the book of my history was Kane and Abel; I so wanted to change my name
- the smell of my history was freshly mowed grass
- the feelings of my history were crisp, complex and courageous
- the teaching of my history was like pulling teeth
- the language of my history was apologetic
- the misunderstanding in my history was tolerance

My history lives on the awakened dreams clouding light;
the sum of my history in shared experiences.

What is Gender?

Gender is complex
Gender is confusing
Gender assigned
Gender ambiguous—male or female
non-binary, neither or both?
Sexual orientation diverse
straight, gay, bisexual, asexual or fluid.
Gender affirmed
Gender identity a personal sense
Gender foisted and confirmed
Gender on the landscape,
amongst the mountains, we climb
and streams we stride through
But this is not who I am
Gender expression
Gender in me

Illustrated by Deb Birks

Trials and Tribulations That a New Year Brings
(Haikus)

Trivia: This year, I will discover the power of colour in therapy
Trauma: Packing away the Christmas Tree and decorations
Triumph: Ordering our new adjustable bed

Trivia

>Cosmic rays surround
>Conscious and subconsciously
>Visible lights shone

Trauma

>Christmas packed away
>Trauma absorbed patiently
>As the loft lid shuts

Triumph

>Dreams of comfort lay
>In the adjustable bed
>I'm in control now

To Do One's Best

To do one's best had never been enough,
so 'to do one's best' was engraved on my back;
in an unrecognisable Chinese symbol for perseverance,
I was aged thirty, without care or benevolence.
In total distraction, my adrenalin did rush,
I felt different, in a state of disguise, I'd blush.
Only I knew the tattoo's true meaning,
a result of my mental demise and deep internal screening.

I was alone, afraid and broken at times,
this symbol now a reminder of the unspoken crimes.
I felt connected and able to weather the storm,
deciding it was now time for the tattoo to transform,
into a unique and prominent tree of life.
That more accurately reflected my continued strife.
It signalled vitality, strength, growth and peace,
each leaf significant in happiness and relief.

Contented

Aesthetic Taste Buds

Have you ever looked at a piece of ART
and felt insecure?
because you don't have
the historical or academic knowledge? Remember
to look and appreciate it scholarly—
the ART world needs people
who are prepared to ask questions properly;
and to be encouraged, gain confidence
rather than making a mockery.

Beauty is about familiarity.
Our aesthetic taste buds change parity,
unlike oral taste buds themselves
which just change position like books on shelves.
It's easy to slag off ART than eulogise it.
Does repeated exposure make you like it?
Would you buy Cezannes card players
worth $260 million if you could?

Apparently, paintings are proven to sell better
when primary colours are the trendsetters.
Whether it's framed in a gallery
to earn the artist a salary
or depicted a masterpiece and placed in a museum.
I can picture it now in Sheffield's Lyceum.
ART is a desire to make things and express oneself—
taste with your eyes and have faith in yourself,
for anything can be ART, but not everything is.

What is ART?

Art is a trance.
Art is tasting with your eyes.
Art is a cherry fragrance.
Art is wearing a woolly jumper.
Art is loose faded jeans and purple platform shoes.
Art is survival.
Art is laughter lines burnt into your skin.
Art is an exercise to paint clear common sense.
Art is a solution.
Art is thinking outside of the box.
Art is a palette of healing.
Art is a train.
Art is squinting at the sun.
Art is ART.

How to Paint a Picture Postcard of Paradise

We despair at a wrong brush stroke or rogue bristled hair,
yet rectifying a mistake simply shows that you care.
I think outside of the box, my palette a reservoir of healing;
kaleidoscope skies, immersed tones so appealing.

I allow my brush to wander wet on wet;
injections of colour from my paralysed pipette.
An endless flat horizon outlined in pencil,
like watered-down gravy used with a stencil.
Splash and splosh as the crisp waves land,
then the slap and suck of water on sand.

Small circles of soft white foam coil around the peaceful rocks,
as the rhythmic eyes flick and lazily mock.
As if in a trance, my unblinking blue eyes,
sweep over the canvas where paradise lies.
A beach bathed in dawn's first rays,
framed effortlessly under the turquoise haze.

Now my painting can talk back at me and empathise emotionally;
having seen the paint, brush and canvas collaborate collectively.
Art is about tasting with our eyes.
Imagination translated—any form, any size,
framed effortlessly under the turquoise haze.

Now my painting can talk back at me and empathise emotionally;
having seen the paint, brush and canvas collaborate collectively.
Art is about tasting with our eyes.
Imagination translated—any form, any size.

Colours I Believe In

What colour do I need in order to believe?

- cerulean to create healthy routines
- ultramarine to unlock the power of proximity
- purple to practise self-love
- crimson to change my perspective
- forest green to feed my mind with positivity
- magenta to master self-confidence
- cobalt to change focus
- teal to take credit for achievements
- peach to practise gratitude
- ebony to embrace strengths and weaknesses equally
- chocolate to consciously adopt limiting beliefs
- and fandango to face fears.

My Purple Dm's

When I wear my purple boots,
I speak my mind.
When I pick blackberries
I leave a trail of footprints behind.
When I grow beetroot,
I have no need to count calories.
When I wear amethyst,
it speaks power as I parade as an activist.
I am both rebellious and zealous,
in my fave purple boots,
that are Dr Martens, no less.

When I wear my purple boots,
I know I can trust you.
I can rely upon you,
like favoured royalty.
A masterpiece in acrylics,
demonstrates my creativity.
I have the personality of a longhorn beetle;
cryptically coloured to avoid detection,
where hiding is no exception
in my fave purple boots,
that are Dr Martens, no less.

When I wear my purple boots,
there's an air of mystery about me,
A poetic and artistic realm of fantasy.
I'm an example of femininity with nervous shoots,
associated self-expression and obsessions I'll dispute.
I speak out about what I believe in,
anxiety evoked under my skin,
until I find answers confirming the absolute.
My identity is mirrored,
in my fave purple boots,
that are Dr Martens, no less.

When I wear my purple boots,
I acknowledge their iconic heritage.
I'm customised as a classic,
contextualised and specialised.
Their yellow welt stitching revitalised
and speciality leather symbolised.

I wear my own attitude and identity,
never question my depression
or fight aggression,
when I wear my purple Dr Martens.
One thing I will not do
is gardening
In my fave free-thinking purple boots.

You'll Never Believe What I Can See

You'll never believe what I can see.

- an angry paintbrush because the artist had chosen the wrong colour
- a wooden spoon that couldn't cut, yet left emotional scars
- Richie Sumak appreciating his own toenail collection whilst writing his next manifesto
- Will Smith using onomatopoeia as a weapon of mental destruction
- Beyonce building sandcastles on Elton John's Yellow Brick Road
- large chunks of washing up on the beach
- a fox in a top hat whispering into the ear of a rabbit
- a tramp pissing in my garden trying to help the plants grow
- trees gossiping about the people who have worked under them
- a glass that was neither half empty or half full, so I drank it!
- Putin purchasing a baby clown from the Russian terrorist black market
- my mother dancing because all of the socks from the tumble dryer matched up
- tumbleweed refusing to tumble but more willing to prowl

No need to see it, but what I do believe is that you should never take advice from someone who thinks that red paint dries quicker than blue paint.

Mellow Yellow

Yellow is intelligent, collecting wisdom as she ages.
Her happiness reflected like summertime cricket.
Yellow looks like dancing daffodils and sunflowers smiling at the sun.
Yellow hears the honey-drunken bees and laughter amongst friends.
Yellow tastes the citric acid of lemons rasping on throaty stairways.
Yellow smells of traditional butterscotch fudge and the shelf-life of bananas.
Yellow is complex,
awakened with confidence and optimism.
Yellow is hypnotised by mellow tones,
tempered by maturity, ready to clone
Yellow likes a challenge
creating enthusiasm for life.
Yellow custard graces the apple pie.
Yellow cheese accompanies tipsy wine evenings.
Yellow pineapple rings sit upon slices of 'Little Pig'
Yellow bell peppers and sweet mangoes on the shopping list.
Yellow corn combined by the harvester.
Yellow borrows the success from yesterday
And takes it forward into tomorrow.
Yellow is power and fulfilment in abundance;
courage and self-esteem her comfort.
Yellow is the energetic happiness in a highly-coiled spring.
BOING! Yellow is invested in me.

I had just spied what I thought was a Chameleon amongst a number of other soft toys in the local garden centre. Surely not, who would buy one of those for a child? I didn't need an excuse for I had fallen in love with yet another meaningful character. I called him Colin.

My Name is Colin, the Chameleon

Colin sits on my desk staring at me with his Kermit eyes;
he definitely can't see what is ahead of him!
Huge white gobstoppers, each marked with a black spot sit on either side.
I never expected to find a chameleon who sat on his arse all day,
but mine does with his spiral Cumberland sausage tail.
He's got two legs with four toes and two arms with four fingers.
I doubt they are actually called fingers and toes though!
He has a two-tone pink tuft on his helmet head;
it looks more like a Mohican than ornamentation.
His two nostrils aren't quite aligned correctly with my eye line
but neither is his wrinkled chin keeping his mouth firmly shut.
He's spotted within his own camouflaged skin,
not spots just dabbed on like a ladybird pin.
He looks quite sad as I take another look at him.
God knows what he thinks of me.
I must remember to pay for him at the till.
Whereupon paying
The cashier started saying,
"You know he's got proper 'yoke toed' toes
on his zygodactylous feet."
I simply nodded, paid and left
with him tucked under my arm
noticing he had his mouth shut too.

Factory Made

Family is a factory where humans are made,
where the colour of love appears,
ancestry kindred and pedigree no less.

An invention we are not.
A new font, baseline, seedbed or speciality neither
BUT part of a generation as in production.
The years between parents and children,
regardless of what we look like,
want to be like or feel like.

Family strengths place care and commitment first,
appreciation and affection second,
positive communication third
and time together fourth.
A sense of spiritual well-being fifth,
trusting yourself and others sixth,
empathy seventh
and adaptivity eighth.

Learning is not a dot-to-dot model,
family is one of nature's masterpieces.

Springtime

Springtime
April showers
life, rebirth, joy and love
Plants begin to grow, flowers bloom
Clocks change

I Saw the Lambs... After a poem by Thomas Hardy: I Watched a Blackbird

I saw the lambs leaping, head-butting and running around with friends.
One Sunday morning,
out of the coach window.
I watched pastures increase with innocent born;
sweet, meek, new life close to their mothers,
suckling from their teats in between nips of grass.
And the sheep's tone and pitch indicates which ewe's lambs were in distress
I got off the coach for an emergency toilet stop.

Lambing

Lambing
Springtime's newborn
One born every minute
limitlessly, innocently
Grazing

'Skeggy' Memories

I rode a donkey.
I remember my brother being washed in the caravan sink,
whilst I sat on the caravan step with my best friend.
Every day in 'Skeggy', we walked through a housing estate (notably with no houses only bungalows), and
past the bingo hall where Nana had usually won the previous night.
We stalled at the 'bookies', whilst Grandad placed his daily bet,
then we ate sausage and chips on a tray for lunch.
We took one look in the 'tat' shops and often walked away,
although we always had time to fill a bag of sweets.
The fairground was active all day, but
we loved the lights and arcades at night,
spending our two pence coins from a cardboard tub.
It always took ages to reach the beach
and my dream would come true,
I rode a donkey.
My brother never did!

Richmond Caravan Park, Skegness

It might have taken three hours to reach the caravan
but it was worth it, even though I wasn't a fan
of the sausage and bacon cobs we stopped off for
on the way.

I literally could not wait to get my roller skates on,
or hire one of those two-person bikes where there
was space for two more people to sit behind you.
In most cases, our teddy bears took the toddler seats upfront,
it was bloody hard work pedalling on my own!

The adventure playground and zip-line were favourites too,
my brother was forced to watch as he was too young.
My grandparents spent hours watching me fly;
that's what I used to say to them, "Come and watch my fly."

In the evening we got dressed up for bingo in the club;
before the disco started—flashing lights galore and songs to dance to
'Hey Mickey' was played several times
A bottle of pop and a bag of crisps was a treat.
We never really stayed for the evening act.

I was more content to play 'Little Brown Jug'
on the mini keyboard, I'd spent all my pocket money on.
I must have driven them mad, but they said they loved me.
Dominoes and card games with the chance to win fifty pence.
I always won!

On-site was the best chippy ever.
I could be trusted with a list of what to get and a tenner.
The change I was allowed to keep for running the errand,
change in two pence coins I always asked the lady for.

We didn't really need to leave the caravan park,
it had more than enough to create nostalgic memories.
I'm just thankful for my grandparents
and for my Aunt Liz who loaned us the van.

Bantering Bees

Listen.
As bees banter
around the honeypot;
sweet and significant scent.
Springtime.

My Maldive Man

Waking up with the ocean at his feet,
he bathed in the lucid, turquoise waters,
whilst she undressed his suitcase.
He laughed with the clownfish,
in a place where nature met heaven.
White sands walking and talking free.

Deliriously
    happy
        with
            his
                love

Towelled dry under the coconut palms,
ready to share breakfast with the Ghives.
He prepares to leave the hut without any shorts!
Because she didn't leave any out!
—A reflection of their fifty shades.
Everything on the island is LOVE

He wore only what he was given.
He'd whisper sweet nothings in her ear.
He'd smell of the salt from the rising humidity and ocean coral,
waiting patiently to swing down from heaven and hug her tightly,
just as he had done before.

Heaven's Reflection

Coloured, conical shapes,
that challenge my perception.
A kaleidoscope—psychedelic and surreal,
scrambled and fractured elements of time,
formations and logistics mapped out.
Rose-coloured glasses are dancing at dawn.
I am 'Heaven's Reflection'.

My Interpretation – What is 'belief'?

When we listen, we believe.
When we acknowledge what we believe, we share.
I am authentic when I believe.
A foundation of beliefs and core values—
all what we care about most.

Credence, credit and faith.
A chance to contemplate.
What has value and worth?
What do I admire most?
What matters most is amongst our roots.

Random Mat

The cat sat on the mat.
A gorgeous Georgian style, with luxurious threads,
that's the mat, not the cat!
It had always been made clear to me that it wasn't one of my beds.
I'd rather a four-poster personally,
with a warm feathered duvet;
like the queen once used.
Soft pillows feathering my bed, a fleecy blanket to
snuggle up to.
It was regal!
It was illegal! That's to sleep in the Queen's bed.
I doubt she'd be happy to sit on my mat.
Anyway, I was forbidden to sit on 'the mat', especially without my hat.
I'd let the king borrow it.

Down the Rabbit Hole

I'm a people pleaser
so down the rabbit hole, I go,
to visit a place only I could imagine;
a place and space
to unpack my self-critics,
alter my thought process
and work out if 'I' should listen or not.

I'm my own detective,
recognising when to take a pause,
acknowledging the power of words—
their intervention, correction and criticism;
recalling words that I'd previously forgotten,
so I make no apologies
before I speak.

I spiral into deep regret.
I berate myself for saying 'yes'
and replay incidents over and over again.
In my mind, I ask myself
whether I should or should not
take battle with my critical inner voice.
I'm trapped and unable to move on.

Only I can accept who I am;
whether I'm worthy of love and respect.
I recall an inventory of negative messages.
I need everyone to like me
even the people I do not know.
I take on the burden of other people's feelings
but an unwillingness to take credit or praise.

I mirror my behaviour
on the person surrounding me,
avoiding any and all conflicts.
I'll happily take the blame when it is not my fault,
I always get second opinions
and ask someone capable to double-check my work.
I agree even when I disagree and apologise too much.
In a bid to resurface and practice saying 'no',
I consider my priorities,
identify any toxic traits,

allow myself time to make decisions,
set healthy boundaries
and rediscover my inner self.
My thought process is now altered
and I know when to listen or not,
so choosing to exit the rabbit hole
that I'd recently entered
was an easy decision.

Blackbird

Blackbird
Its mellow song
Nose like a broken moon
Singing in a remote Welsh wood
After rain

Freedom
—a mirror cinquain

Jazz age
Syncopation
Improvised on the spot
The infectious musical score
patterns

Aged
Rooted in the blues and ragtime
self-expression, rhythms
Jazz a language
Freedom

The 'Box'

On Mel's doorstep is the infamous 'Box';
More precisely the 'Collect and Drop Box',
where new Yarn Bomb projects are collected from stock,
open for business twenty-four hours around the clock.
A lifeline for many during COVID when permitted laws
only enabled the crafters to communicate outdoors.
Daily drops in the 'crate', surveyed if complete
or replacement yarn swapped anonymously discrete.

Every day in Cosby, crafters will bargain and dicker,
in an equinox exchange, crossing yarns celestial equator.
From a listed property, namely 'the barn',
Eureka moments are constructed from all sorts of yarn.
Installations recycled and renewed each year,
via the 'vessel' as busy as summer's Blackpool pier.

The large clear 'receptacle' is a place of safety for returns,
in its 'trunk', a formula of collusion, where emptiness yearns.
As per instructions, under the lid pass a pool of ideas,
inherent from a masterplan, yarn's roadmap under gallerias.
In Cosby, many manoeuvres pass by in the dark,
transactions back and forth, from Village Hall, Victory Park.

Why wait until Monday when our Crafters group meet?
Ask for a ball or packet of wool via Twitter Tweet.
Use the 'box', 'tub', 'holder' whatever you call it,
To either return or collect your crochet or knit.
Don't worry if your work doesn't look like what it should
We've all been there and questioned 'Is it any good?'
Ultimately, the finished products bow to the community,
even if during creation there are elements of lunacy.

Quaker Haikus

I am a Quaker.
This is what it means to me—
'A statement of fact'

What matters most is
personal experience.
All days are precious

The meeting begins
when the first person sits down—
gathering silence

Collective stillness
until moved to stand and speak
in short ministry

Spiritually
inspired resolutions
to change behaviour

We share our blessing—
be still with me in my mind.
Equal importance

No thees or thous heard.
The spirit is god
finding love and truth.

More open-hearted.
Fruits are called 'faith in action'
What is good and true?

Truth means more to us,
motives declare commitment—
try to live simply

Peace is a process
to engage in, not a goal,
just decide to change.

Gardencraft

I cannot see beyond my garden,
yet I am the envy of my neighbourhood.
Winnowing wind drives through my drowsy heart,
no place to shrink into secret shadows.
Looking back at nature's tender ministries,
where early buttercups unfolded,
fields were scattered with clover
and the maturing sunshine spoke
in unison with the peace felt within my breast.
On the windowsill, in the idle summer hours,
the wise thrush sings everything twice.
Our England is a garden,
flinging whiffs of perfume,
whilst vexed meditation pulls at my strings,
driving sleep into my footpath.
Unspoken lavender heads are taught,
where minds are diverted,
words unspoken
and tears of innocence
improvise on the spot.

My Summary of Jamaica

As you hike, Reggae Music can be heard
far, far below competing with the chirp of crickets and katydids.
A myriad of peony wallies flit before you,
signalling their phosphorescent semaphore.

Sea turtles dance their slow ballet in cerulean waters,
amid the darting rainbow-coloured fish.
The sweet smell of ganja smoke still perfumes the breeze,
swaying palms above crystal clear waters.

Inspired By My Own Recovery

Pain took away all of my energy.
I no longer recognised myself.
My confidence crushed
but somehow I never lost hope.
I learnt that I didn't need to fight or fear pain.
I needed to accept and understand it instead.
I now have more determination than ever
to prove to myself 'I can do it'.
Inspired by my own recovery,
I only need to do what I do best
and that's look ahead.

Gender Fluid

Gender is non-binary.
I'm flexible in the sex I identify.
Neither male nor female.
No set place on the gender spectrum.
I'm not confused.
I experiment and
act upon different feelings.
It's a journey to find out who I am.
Hormonal changes.
Physical changes.
Sexual feelings evident.
What am I becoming?
Who am I attracted to?
How do I identify?
Fluidity.
All normal.

This poem is written in the style of Warda Kashif using her poem 'If I Had any Superpower, I Would Want the Power to Control …'

If I Had Any Superpower, I Would Want the Power to Control Smiling

If I had any superpower, I would want the power to control smiling,
to grin, smirk and beam,
to wear a smile that frowns, scowls, and grimaces too,
to be more likeable, courteous, and competent—Eeek!

If I had any superpower, I would want the power to control smiling,
to reduce blood pressure, pain, and stress,
to increase endurance,
to lengthen my overall lifespan.

If I had any superpower, I would want the power to control smiling,
because whether your smile is genuine or not
it sends out the message that 'Life is good' to the brain.
It keeps me healthier.
It drives positivity.
It boosts my self-esteem and confidence.

I'd be happier than hippos.
I'd be healthier than my GP.
I'd be more likeable than the Mona Lisa.
I'd be more courteous than royalty.
I'd be more competent than technology.
All because I'd have the power to control smiling.

Blackberry Picking

A sudden concentration of attention
lifted my mood on a cool autumn evening.
Clusters of blackberries
in all fitness of line and colour,
some blemished, some wrinkled
others perfect.
They rooted through the hedgerows,
hidden in hardy brambles.
An ideal fruit for foraging.
Hands stained purple.
In that moment in time, I had understanding,
for the quality of beauty in fitness remains the same.

Nova, Nova – Supernova

I only know one Nova;
as far as I am aware.
There is only one Nova
in Cosby, Leicestershire.
Her name denotes that
she brings something new,
free space association,
releasing powerful energy too.
But when I think of Nova
fig rolls are not far behind.
When I think of fig rolls
it's Nova my brain reminds.

She's the most fabulous crocheter,
producing marvels week after week;
give her a challenge,
one after another she will seek.
You should see her ballards
created with thought and dexterity.
One particular one to mention
is her Frieda Khala sincerity.
Her imagination is like no other,
the detail in design,
time told inventions;
she's our crafters Queen Mother.

She champions work for charity
and makes surprise creations,
with smiles and laughter to share
including the naked nudity
patterns conjured are sensations.
She doesn't need frills and fluff to feel feminine
maintaining a sweet side that is hard to rival.
She's definitely not just another name,
she'll always stand out with her flambouncy and fame.
She's our powerful illumination of a star,
an explosion of sheer fame,
Nova, Nova Supernova is her name.

A Debut Selection of Poems By Poppy

Fears

When someone asks me what I'm scared of,
I play it basic and say 'the dark'.

Sometimes, I'll say heights,
needles, or even sharks.
Maybe I'll say spiders or
flying away from home.
I'll say confined spaces or
even pain and loud sounds.

But I hide my real fears and put them on a faraway shelf,
because my biggest fear is that you'll see me the way I see myself.

By Poppy

The Rain

She walks alone in the rain,
letting the drops of water run down her face,
mixing with the salty tears
she desperately tries to hold in.
But as those tears are joined with the rain
she feels safe to let them out.
This puts her at ease.
It's almost as if she isn't alone.
The world is crying with her;
she loves the way the sky looks;
as if it's storming,
so dark, dreary and dim.
Just like her mind.

By Poppy

The Reason

I used to believe that everything
happens for a reason,
and then I didn't!
Some things are just painful;
the results of living in the dark,
and the broken world,
and that's the beginning
and the end of it.

I used to believe a lot of things were
forever and never for me.
Impossible.
And dream that I'd lost the chance
to be loved.
I'm not a worthy person so being loved
was the last thing I was looking for.

But I like the idea that you're the reason,
because of how well you love
my broken pieces and sharp edges.
It makes me remember less of
what came before.
It's not like it never happened.
Better than that—
It happened
but sometimes, I forget,
because you've helped me remember
more important things
like how to laugh and
what it feels like to be alive.
Safe and free.

So, whilst I still don't believe
everything happens for a reason—
a phrase that's empty and stale.
In the face of real pain and grief,
I see how the little things,
the choice to do the healing,
the determination to learn to live
led me right to you.

By Poppy

Things Only I Will Ever Know

For eternity,
the most beautiful things
to me
about you
are the things
you won't even know
about yourself.
Things only I know of
because everyday
I read you
like a book
that has never been read.
You're beautiful cover
with your inspiring title
an amazing story
I yearn
to learn
from your mystery.

By Poppy

Trauma Is My Devil

Trauma is my devil,
The cause of all my sins.
It taunts me in the darkness,
with memories from within.

The devil leaves his scars,
as I lie awake with
sleepless nights and fear.
Tiredness and hope disappear.

Morning light is welcome;
the devil disappears.
Time to start living.
And hide all my fears.

People don't see my devil.
My mask is my disguise.
I smile and put on a show.
Hoping no one will know.

By Poppy

Your Eyes

You hated your eye colour;
called it dull and dirty brown.
Wished for the deep blue of an ocean
where admirers' hearts would drown.
And it pained me when I realised
you'd never see it like I do.
The way your eyes hint at a story
that I want to read right through.
They hold specks of stolen sunlight
that you'd miss with just one glance.
And a depth of raw emotion
that can freeze you in a trance.
There's a fix of melted chocolate
when I'm craving something sweet,
but a hold like that's so unwavering,
that I find it hard to meet.
I fall right down the rabbit hole
when I look into your eyes.
The brown of Earth's unfettered beauty
that I yearn to memorise.
When I was tired of not belonging,
they made me feel like I'd been found.
And I hope you never say again,
that your eyes are simply brown.

By Poppy